bubblefacts...

WORLD WONDERS

MILES KELLY
PUBLISHING

First published in 2005 by
Miles Kelly Publishing Ltd
Bardfield Centre, Great Bardfield, Essex, CM7 4SL

Copyright © Miles Kelly Publishing Ltd 2005

2 4 6 8 10 9 7 5 3 1

Publishing Director:
Anne Marshall

Senior Editor:
Belinda Gallagher

Editorial Assistant:
Hannah Todd

Designer:
Louisa Leitao

Cartoons:
Mark Davis

Production:
Estela Boulton

ISBN 1-84236-534-7

Printed in China

Library of Congress Cataloging-in-Publication Data
is on file at the Library of Congress.

Indexer: Jane Parker

www.mileskelly.net
info@mileskelly.net

Contents

Ancient wonders

antique marvels

The Romans built a massive stadium for deadly duels. The Colosseum was a giant stone stadium that held crowds of 50,000 people. Emperors and other rich Romans paid for "games" that included gladiator battles and prisoner fights with wild beasts.

The Colosseum was opened in AD80. The lighthouse at Alexandria was 330 ft (100 m) tall with a fire on top.

The Great Sphinx is a huge statue of a half-man, half-lion that guards the pyramids at Giza, Egypt. It probably shows the dead king Khafre as a man with the power of a lion.

A Babylonian king built a fountain shaped garden for his queen. It had many levels and spectacular plants.

Slaves kept the hanging Gardens of Babylon well-watered. The Sphinx was carved 4,500 years ago.

Amazing Americas

go west!

The Egyptians were not the only people to build pyramids. Some pyramid-builders lived in Central and South America. Instead of using them as tombs, the Incas, the Maya, and the Aztecs used their pyramids as temples.

Can you believe it?

Explorers searched for a mystery city where everything was said to be made of gold.

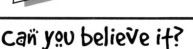

WHAT'VE YOU GOT TO LOOK SO HAPPY ABOUT?

WHAT?!

ARE WE NEARLY DONE YET?

The Incas built a mountaintop city called Machu Picchu. It was rediscovered in 1911 after 400 years.

Building pyramids was hard work. The Nazca people scratched huge pictures on the desert floor.

In Mexico, pyramids were dedicated to the Sun and Moon. A city in Peru was built from mud compounds.

African marvels

mud and mosques

Nigeria was a great center of metalwork wonders. The Benin Empire was founded in the 11th century AD and was famous for its brass sculptures. Benin City, the capital, survived until 1897, when the British destroyed it, taking thousands of statues.

CUT THE NOISE OUT!

BIG IMPROVEMENT!

ARRRGGH!

EEK! A SCARY YELLOW-HEADED MONSTER!

In Cameroon, people built pyramid-shaped houses with roofs made from long bamboo stalks.

In the Middle Ages, a powerful African nation built an impressive stone city as its center in Zimbabwe.

Mali has a mosque built from mud. The Dogon tribe of Mali built their houses in the shape of people.

Temple lands

the Lion's Mouth

King Kashyapa ruled from inside a lion. The Sri Lankan king's mountain fortress was known as Sigiriya, or Lion's Mouth, because it could only be reached by climbing through well-guarded gates, carved in the shape of a lion's gaping jaw.

I NEED THE BATHROOM!

I KNOW HIS BREATH SMELLS, JUST DON'T BREATHE IN!

HAS HE TRIED FLOSSING?

CHARMING!

DOES SHE DO ANYTHING ELSE?

The Lion's Mouth was built high on a small plateau. The city of Pagan once had 4,000 Buddhist shrines.

Angkor Wat was the biggest temple ever built. The Khmer kingdom in Cambodia was believed to be ruled by god-kings. Their capital at Angkor contained a huge complex of buildings, with artificial lakes, moats, and long boundary walls covered in carvings.

We still can't crack a code of writing on 4,000 year-old tablets from the Harappa Empire in India.

Angkor Wat was saved after the kingdom collapsed. Buddhists built a huge stone shrine in Borobudur.

Eastern splendors

a great wall!

One wall is 3,980 mi (6,400 km) long. Chinese civilization was based on farming, and the young Chinese nation was often raided by nomads from the North. From 214BC onwards, China built a stone wall along the border to keep its neighbors out.

The Great Wall of China was made by joining together smaller walls that earlier emperors had built.

The wall was 30 ft (9 m) high, with watchtowers positioned along its length. Guards patrolled the wall as it was being built, so that workers did not have to worry about being attacked. If a worker died, his body was built into the wall.

The top of the wall was paved with stones or bricks, but the wall itself was built from soil and rubble. The outside was covered with stone slabs to make it strong. Peasants and criminals were forced to work on the wall because a great deal of man power was required.

If enemies attacked, a fire was lit on top of the nearest watchtower to warn people of the danger.

Mighty monuments
sacred places

Stone giants on Easter Island weigh as much as 1,000 men. Giant stone statues, called moai, frightened the first European visitors to Easter Island in the Pacific Ocean. The biggest of the 600 figures weighs at least 75 tons. Carved from single blocks of stone, the statues were moved great distances before being placed to mark tombs.

HELLLOOO OUT THERE!

WHY THE LONG FACE?

AVOCADO SOUP ANYONE?

YESS! YESS! YESS!

CRACKLE! SNAP!

STONY SILENCE!

The Easter Island statues had eyes of coral. Ancient Britons built a sacred stone circle at Stonehenge.

Stonehenge was made with giant stones, some of which were brought 240 mi (385 km) from a quarry in Wales. They were arranged so that the Sun shone into the entranceway on the morning of the longest day of summer— the summer solstice.

One giant mound in Britain is a total mystery. The same ancient Britons who built Stonehenge also built a mysterious hill. Silbury Hill near Avebury, is another stone circle, but its purpose is unknown. It is 130 ft (40 m) tall and 98 ft (30 m) across at the top. There is no sign of a tomb inside.

French holy men went on long religious parades. Maltese farmers once worshiped fertility goddesses.

Watery cities!
beneath the ocean

Ancient cities have been swallowed by the sea. The sea level in the Mediterranean has changed since cities began to be built around it. The Black Sea coastline was pushed back at a speed of over 0.5 mi (1 km) a day when the Mediterranean began to pour in, 7,500 years ago.

The ancient Greeks told stories of an island called Atlantis that was lost beneath the Atlantic Ocean.

Off the southernmost island of Japan, a stone mound has been found with what could be steps and a roadway. It looks like an Inca temple, but geologists say that the features could be explained by the effect of waves smashing against the rock.

There are Roman columns in Italy that have been nibbled by shellfish. This proves they were underwater at some point!

Scientists think that they may have found a lost city 1,970 ft (600 m) under the sea near Cuba.

Undersea vents feed spooky creatures. Almost all life on Earth depends on the Sun to provide energy. But undersea vents feed some very strange-looking life forms. They give off clouds of hot water that contain minerals. These feed tiny plants and animals.

Rat tail fish

The deepest place in the sea is the Mariana Trench. Some parts of it are 7 mi (11 km) below sea level.

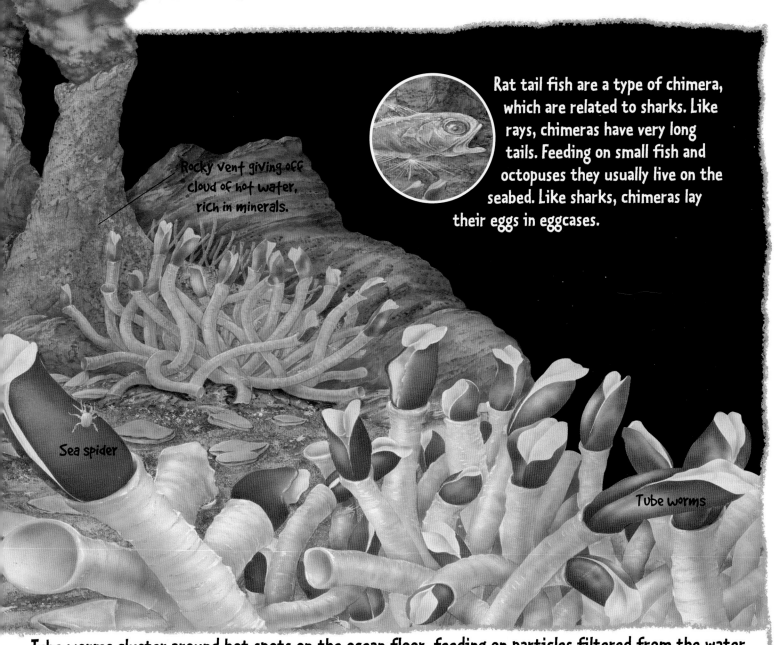

Rocky vent giving off cloud of hot water, rich in minerals.

Rat tail fish are a type of chimera, which are related to sharks. Like rays, chimeras have very long tails. Feeding on small fish and octopuses they usually live on the seabed. Like sharks, chimeras lay their eggs in eggcases.

Sea spider

Tube worms

Tube worms cluster around hot spots on the ocean floor, feeding on particles filtered from the water.

Amazing animals

wonderful nature

The monarch butterfly flies 1,864 mi (3,000 km). Monarch butterflies in North America swarm together for a winter holiday. They fly from colder northern areas down to the forests of southern California and Mexico. In spring they return some of the way, lay their eggs and die. Their young continue the trip north for summer.

Twice a year on Christmas Island, red forest-living crabs migrate in huge swarms to the seashore.

The Great Barrier Reef runs along the northeast coast of Australia for 1,243 mi (2,000 km). It is built and renewed by billions of tiny coral polyps, each one less than 0.4 in (1 cm) across.

Sea creatures often produce millions of eggs, because so many are eaten by hungry predators.

The Great Barrier Reef is visible from space. Termites build huge, oddly shaped mounds as homes.

Rocky situation!

stone me!

The rock of Uluru changes color through the day. The huge lump of rock stranded in Australia's outback is a sacred site for Aborigines. Once known as Ayers Rock, the reddish sandstone goes through amazing color changes at sunrise and sunset.

YAHOO!

YOU'VE LOST YOUR BOOMERANG!

I HATE THESE OUTBACK SPORTS.

C'MON SKIPPY, I'M NOT LETTING GO!

Uluru has lots of small caves around its base, many of which are covered with Aboriginal paintings.

American Indians believed that a rainbow had been turned to stone when they visited the Rainbow Bridge in Utah. The sandstone bridge can appear lavender, pink, or red in sunlight.

There is a desert of white sand in New Mexico. Rare white lizards and mice have evolved to blend in with the white background.

Malaysia is home to a huge cave 328 ft (100 m) wide. Rainbow Bridge changes color in different lights.

Volcano power

bubbling under

Volcanoes can make neat pavements. The Giant's Causeway in Ireland was formed by a volcano's lava flow. It cooled slowly, cracking from the surface downward like drying mud, to form six-sided stone "logs." Irish tradition says that it was built by a giant who wanted to make a road to Scotland.

HELLO DOWN THERE!

BE QUIET!

COME BACK! YOU DIDN'T PAY THE TOLL!

EEK!

Some stone columns of Giant's Causeway are 20 ft (6 m) high. Mount Fuji is visible from 62 mi (100 km) away.

Pilgrims visit the volcano of Fuji. Mount Fuji is Japan's biggest mountain—the result of thousands of eruptions of ash and lava. The shrines that circle the lip of the volcano's crater are home to young trainee priests of the Shinto religion. Mount Fuji last erupted in 1707.

You can enjoy a concert in a lava bubble. As lava flows from a volcano, it cools from the outside, forming hard rock, while the center remains liquid. Sometimes this leaves a cave inside the rock. At Cueva de los Verdes, in the Canary Islands, caves like these have been converted to make a concert hall.

Lava bubbles can create caves. Heat from below ground can heat water, making it burst upward.

Wonder falls!

go with the flow

Niagara Falls is moving upriver. The flowing water eats away the rock below it, causing the lip of the falls to collapse. The waterfall then moves back. Niagara Falls has moved about 3.3 ft (1 m) a year for the last 300 years. It has stabilized now because the Niagara River is redirected at night to hydro-electric power stations.

Niagara Falls was formed about 12,000 years ago when ice melted and made the Niagara River overflow.

Lake Baikal, in Russia, is unusual because it is home to the world's only freshwater seals.

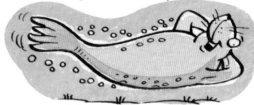

One waterfall is nearly 0.6 ft (1 km) tall. Hidden away in the Venezuelan rain forest is a mountain with steep cliffs. The Angel Falls flow over the edge of one of these cliffs, and drop 3,212 ft (979 m) through the air to the river below.

Angel Falls is the tallest waterfall in the world. Iguaçu Falls creates numerous rainbows with its spray.

The Sydney Opera House was built twice. The weird shapes of the roof were so far ahead of their time that builders had to start work before the materials had even been invented. When the builders realized that the roof would be heavier than expected, they had to blow up the foundations and start again!

The Skydome stadium in Canada has a record-breaking sunroof. The Sydney Opera House has five theaters.

The white cladding on the shells of the Sydney opera House is built from one million ceramic tiles!

You can surf on a beach with a roof in Japan. The Seagaia Ocean Dome is an artificial indoor beach, with a sliding roof. Visitors can surf on artificial waves all year round. The 984 ft- (300 m-) long building is 328 ft (100 m) from the actual coast.

BLING! BLING! BLING!

INDOOR SURFING, IT'S FAR OUT, MAN!

WHIZZZZ! BANG! WHIZZZ!

France has a huge cinema with a screen 49 ft (15 m) high. Disney World employs 45,000 members of staff.

Reach for the sky way up high!

The tallest towers are twins.

The Petronas Towers in Kuala Lumpur are among the world's tallest buildings, at 1,483 ft (452 m) high. They were built for Malaysia's national oil company. There are 88 storys of offices, held up by 16 concrete pillars in each tower.

There are 76 lifts in the Petronas Towers. The Korowai people of Indonesia build their houses in trees.

In Las Vegas a rollercoaster travels around a skyscraper. The Eiffel Tower in Paris is popular with tourists.

Some skyscrapers "dance" or move in the wind! The first skyscraper was built in Chicago 120 years ago.

Index